CANADA

Written by Esta Saint-Claire

COUNTRIES of the WORLD

PowerKiDS press

Published in 2025
by The Rosen Publishing Group, Inc.
2544 Clinton Street, Buffalo, NY 14224

Written by: Esta Saint-Claire
Edited by: Elise Carraway
Designed by: Miranda Tremere

Cataloging-in-Publication Data

Names: Saint-Claire, Esta.
Title: Canada / Esta Saint-Claire.
Description: Buffalo, NY : PowerKids Press, 2025. | Series: Countries of the world | Includes glossary and index.
Identifiers: ISBN 9781499447125 (pbk.) | ISBN 9781499447132 (library bound) | ISBN 9781499447149 (ebook)
Subjects: LCSH: Canada--Juvenile literature.
Classification: LCC F1008.2 S256 2025 | DDC 971--dc23

Manufactured in the United States of America

CPSIA Compliance Information: Batch #CSPK25. For further information contact Rosen Publishing at 1-800-237-9932.

Find us on

Image Credits

All images are courtesy of Shutterstock.com, unless otherwise specified. With thanks to Getty Images, Thinkstock Photo and iStockphoto. Cover – f11photo, Shawn.ccf, Cindy Creighton, Anna Kosheleva, GoodStudio. 2 – kavram. 4–5 – Andrew Minsk, mikecphoto. 6–7 – Mumemories, karamysh, JFunk. 8–9 – Jpiks, FamVeld. 10–11 – Rohit Seth, GTW. 12–13 – Vlad G, Ground Picture. 14–15 – Scott Heaney, Petr Kahanek, Smit. 16–17 – len4foto, TeodorLazarev. 18–19 – Iurii Osadchi, Rob Hainer. 20–21 – Louno Morose, New Africa. 22–23 – Marius M. Grecu, Drakuliren, Anan Kaewkhammul, photomaster, FER737NG.

CONTENTS

Words that look like <u>this</u> can be found in the glossary on page 24.

WHERE IS CANADA?

Canada is in the continent of North America. It is next to the United States and is the second-largest country in the world.

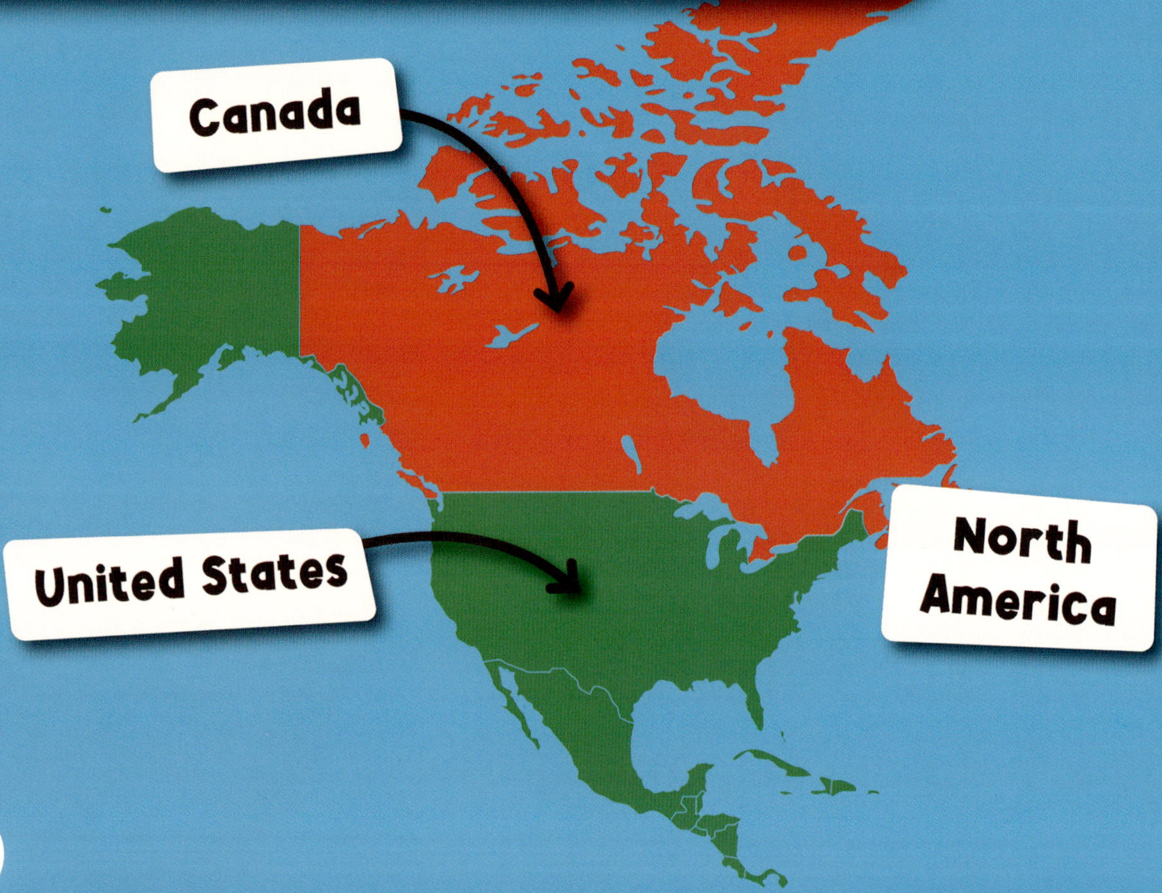

The population of Canada is over 38 million. The capital city of Canada is called Ottawa.

LANDSCAPE AND WEATHER

During the winter, the weather in Canada can be very cold. There is often lots of snow. The weather is usually warmer during the summertime.

Canada is home to many amazing landscapes, such as mountains and coastlines.

Canada is also home to thousands of lakes!

RELIGION

The religion with the most followers in Canada is Christianity. People who follow Christianity are called Christians.

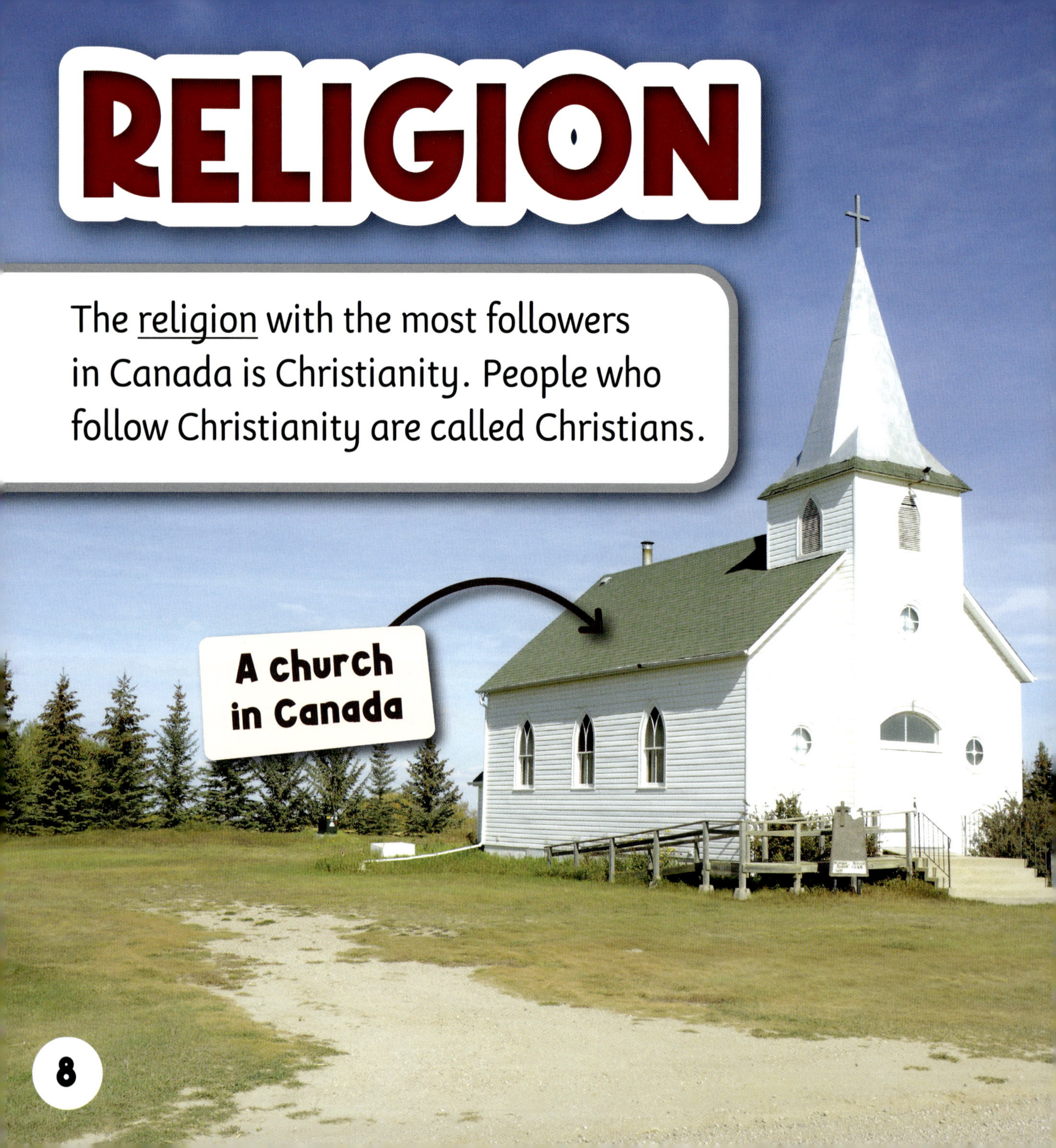

A church in Canada

Other people in Canada follow religions such as Islam, Hinduism, and Buddhism. Many people in Canada do not follow any religion at all.

FAMILIES

Parents and children usually live together in Canada. In some cases, grandparents live with the family too.

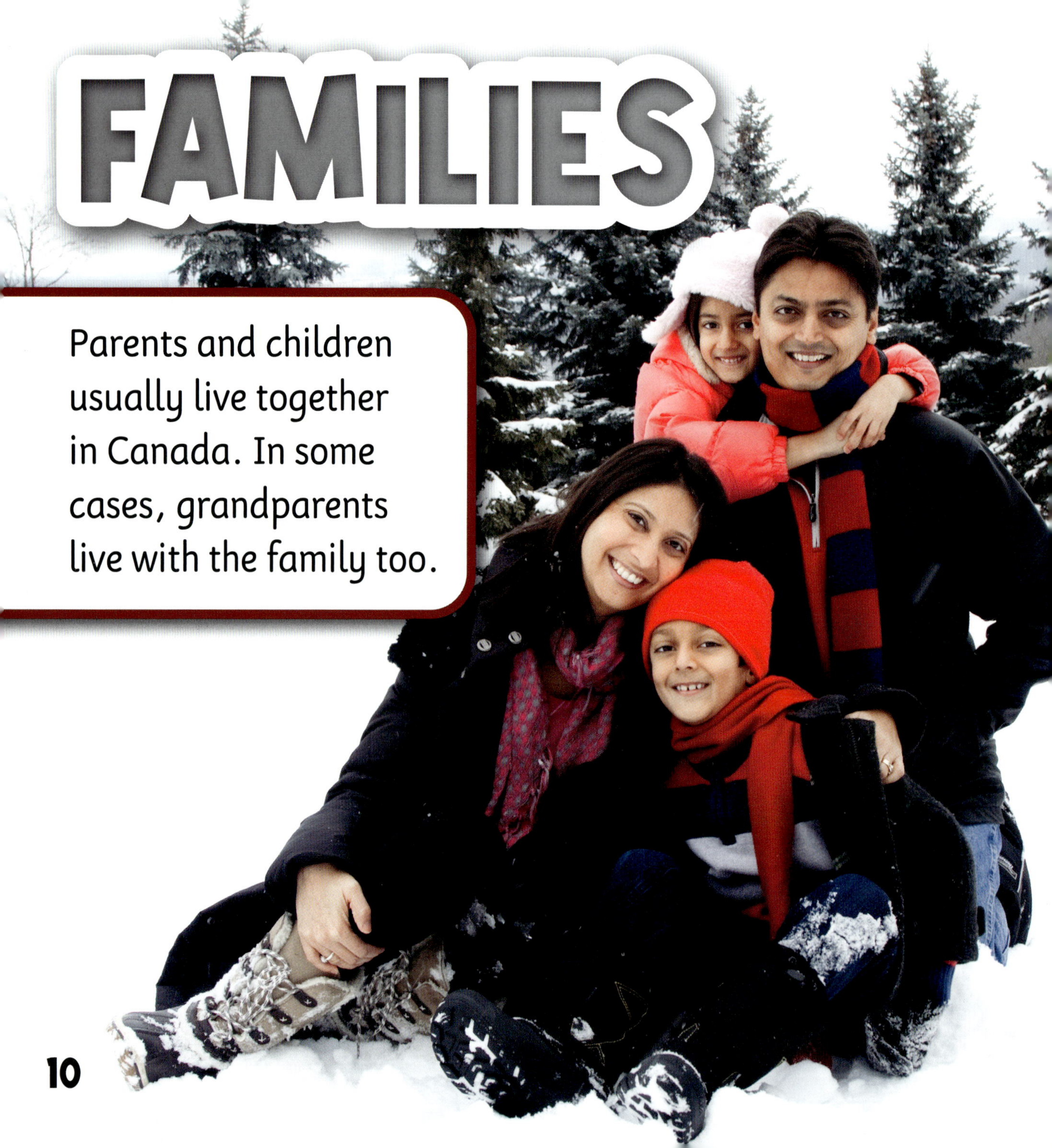

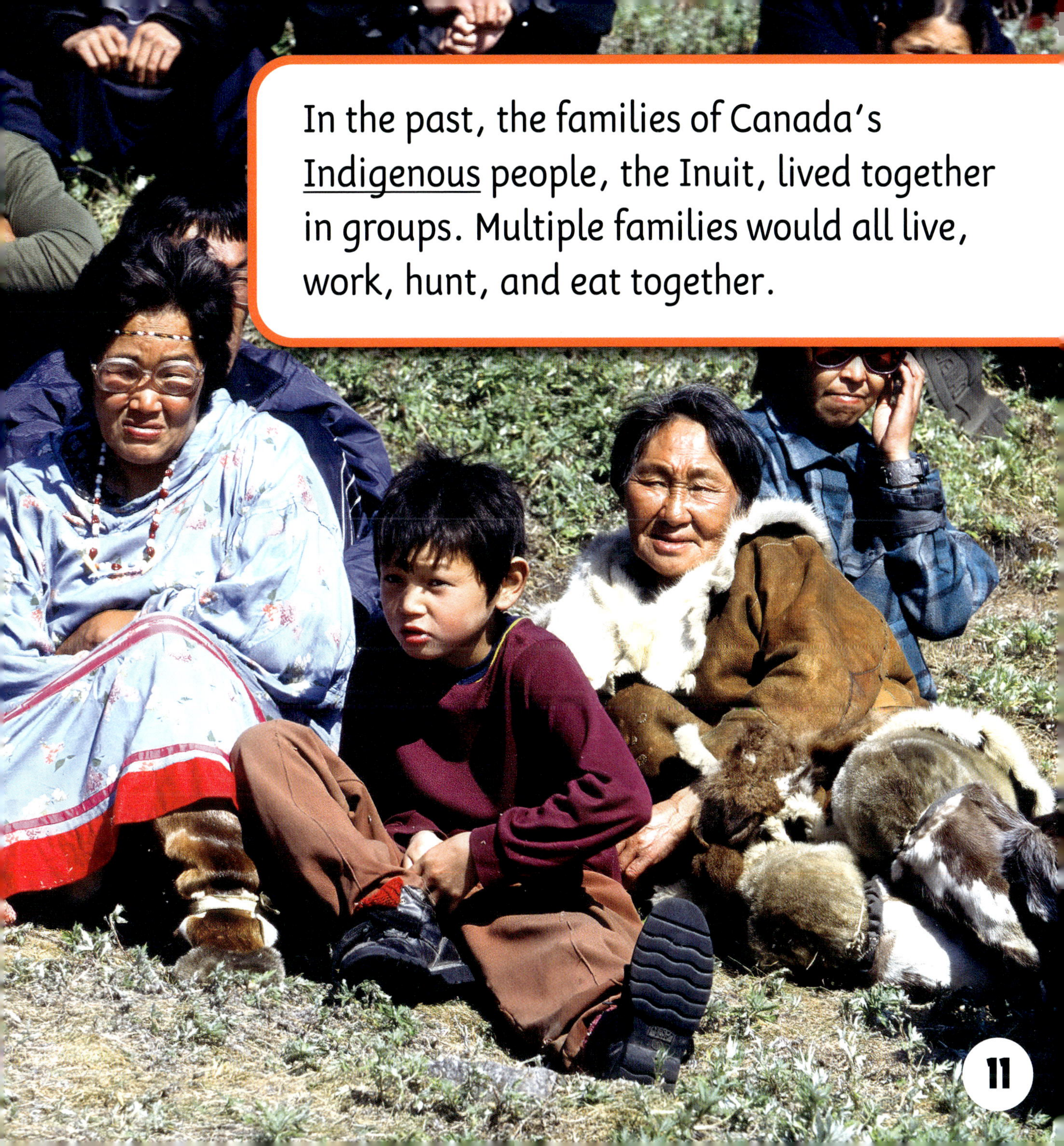

In the past, the families of Canada's Indigenous people, the Inuit, lived together in groups. Multiple families would all live, work, hunt, and eat together.

SCHOOL

Children in Canada start school when they are 5 years old and usually finish when they are 18.

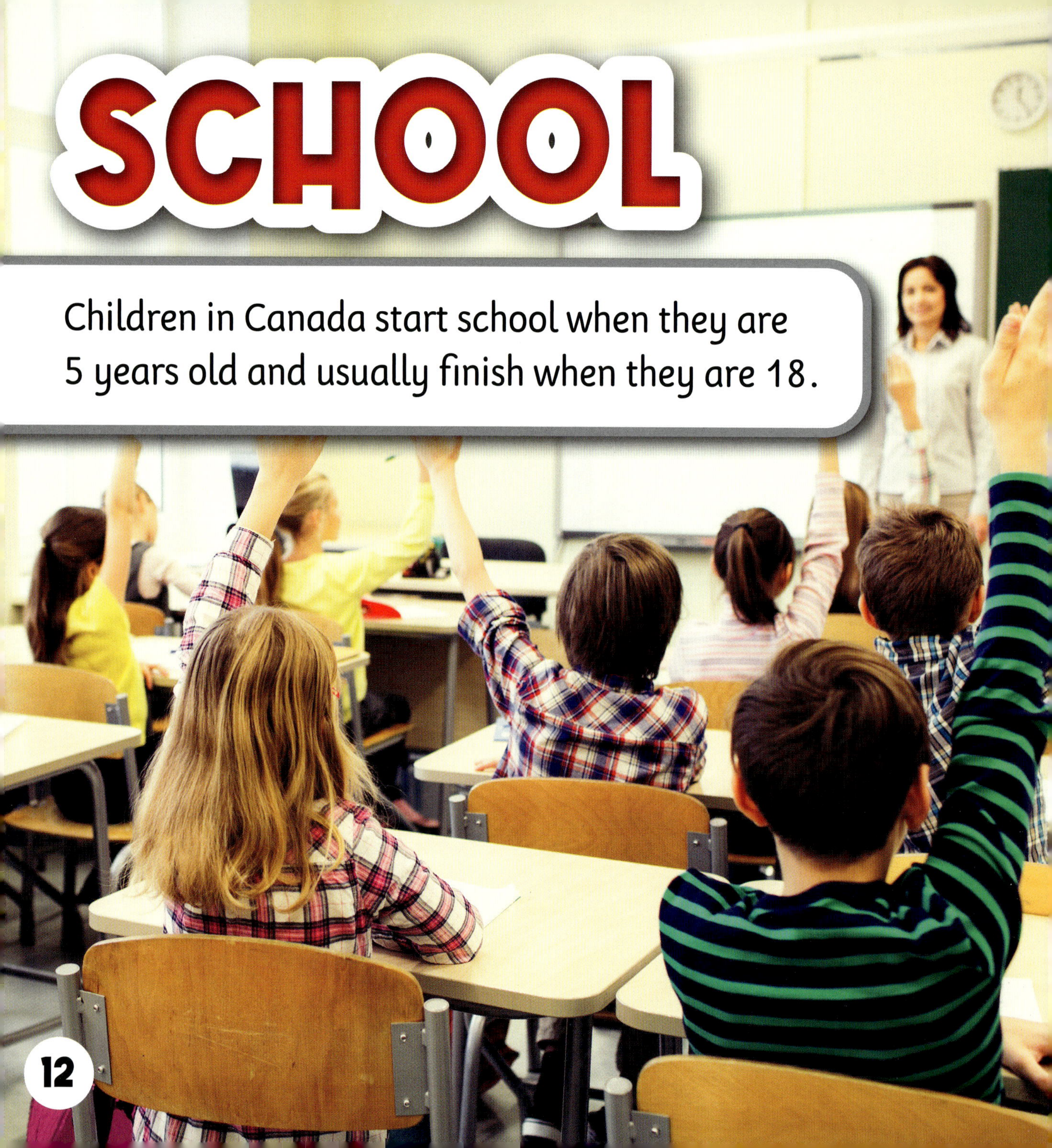

Children in Canada are often encouraged to do activities outside of school, such as sports and art.

When there is snow, children can go skiing!

HOME

Most people in Canada live in towns and cities in the southern part of the country. This is because the weather is usually warmer in the south.

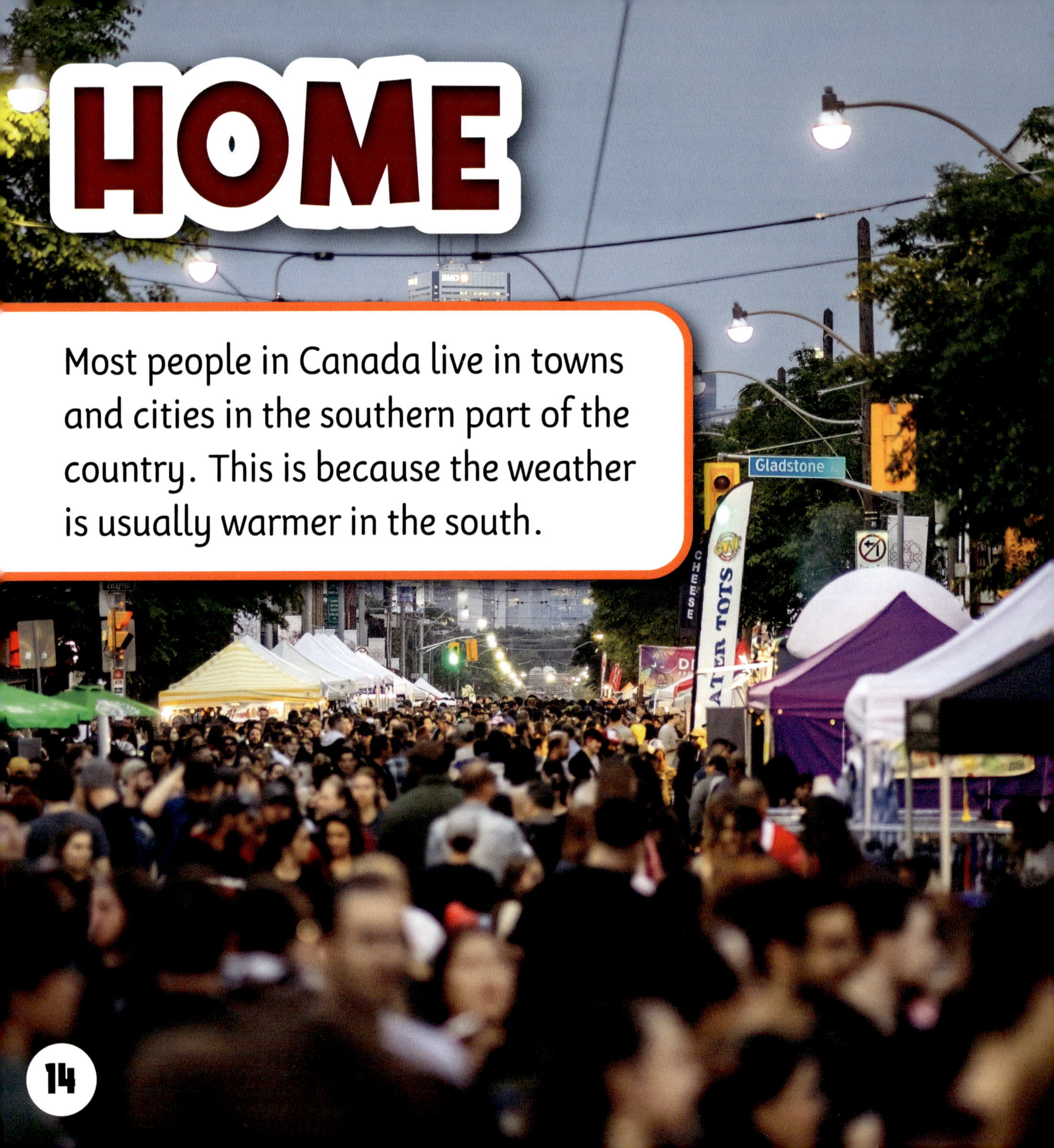

The northern areas of the country are home to the Indigenous Inuit people, although many of them live in cities in the south too. In the past, some Inuit people lived in ice houses called igloos.

CLOTHING

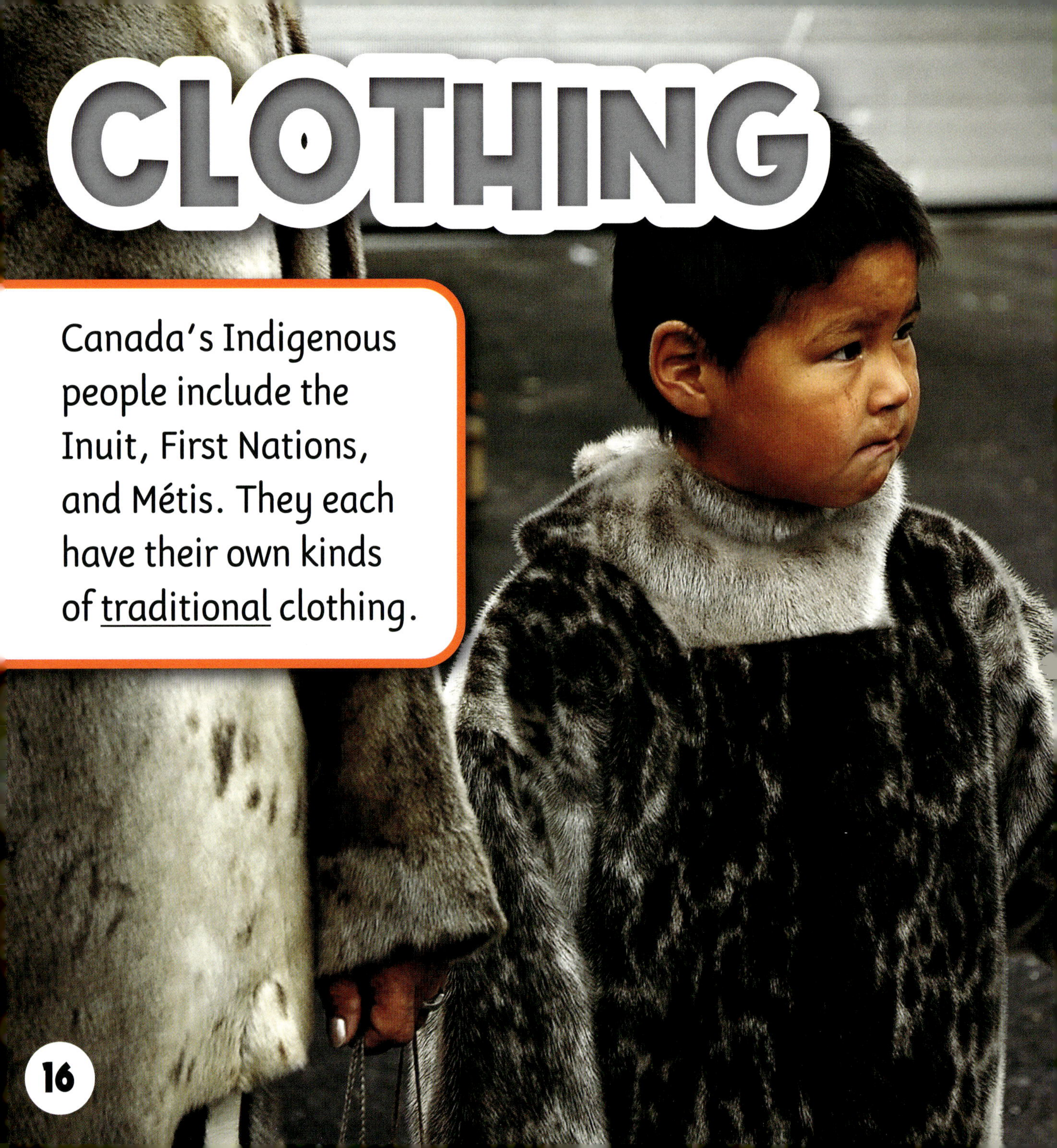

Canada's Indigenous people include the Inuit, First Nations, and Métis. They each have their own kinds of <u>traditional</u> clothing.

Most people in Canada wear comfortable clothing that is suited for the weather.

SPORTS

The national winter sport of Canada is ice hockey. The sport involves two teams of six players and a small disk, called a puck. Each team tries to hit the puck into their opponents' net.

The national summer sport of Canada is lacrosse. The sport involves using a long stick with a net on the end to throw a ball into the opponents' net.

FOOD

Poutine is the national dish of Canada. It is made with French fries that are covered in gravy and cheese curds.

Maple syrup is also popular in Canada. This sweet sauce is often eaten with pancakes or waffles.

FUN FACTS

Canada has the longest coastline of any country in the world!

There are two main languages in Canada: French and English.

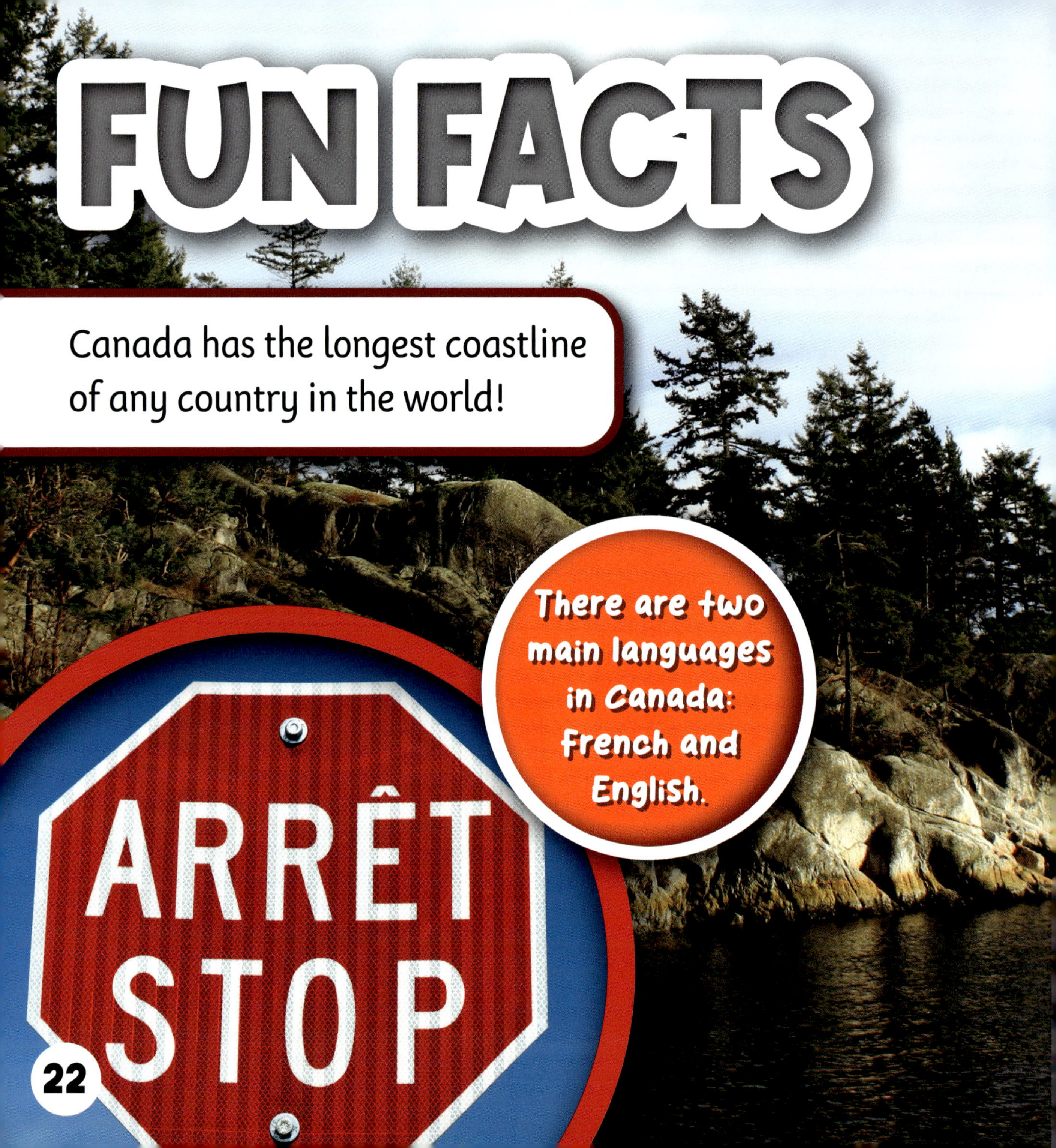

Canada is home to many amazing animals, such as cougars, wolves, and moose.

GLOSSARY

coastlines areas where land meets the sea

continent a very large area of land that is usually made up of many countries

Indigenous having to do with the first people to live in a land

national having to do with things that are shared by or important to people in a country

population the number of people living in a place

religion a system of faith and worship, especially to do with a god or gods

traditional to do with beliefs, customs, or ways of behaving that have been around for a long time

INDEX